The BabyBird Guide
to Stress Disorders:
A Healing Path for PTSD

Heather Silvio, PsyD

Physical edition published in the United States by Panther Books, with permission of original digital publisher BabyBird Guide LLC.

Contact the print publisher at:
information@pantherbooks.us

Contact the author at:
hlsilvio@yahoo.com

ALSO BY HEATHER SILVIO

Happiness by the Numbers:
9 Steps to Authentic Happiness

Not Quite Famous:
A Romantic Comedy of an Actress on the Edge

Beyond the Abyss:
Tales of the Supernatural

Courting Death

A GUIDE TO THE GUIDE

Acknowledgments   i

1   Why the BabyBird Guide   1

2   Trauma Occurs in Many Places and Ways   5

3   Posttraumatic Stress Disorder   7

4   Do You See Yourself in the Symptoms of PTSD   17

5   Specific Techniques to Try   23

6   Nobody Exists in a Vacuum   37

7   Let's Bottom Line It   41

8   Further Reading & Resources   45

ACKNOWLEDGMENTS

A huge thank you to Tanya White of BabyBird Guide for the original digital publication of this book.

1 WHY THE BABYBIRD GUIDE

The BabyBird Guides are designed to provide just the right amount of information needed to learn about a topic, without overwhelming our readers with too many mind-boggling details. The tagline for BabyBird Guide, Knowledge in Bite-Sized Pieces™, conveys our goal to deliver information in easy to consume portions, allowing you to learn one topic at a time, quickly and easily.

The BabyBird Guide to Stress Disorders will provide information specific to Posttraumatic Stress Disorder (PTSD) including what it is, when it occurs, and techniques for minimizing its effects.

The poet Alfred Tennyson, in his play *The Foresters* (later named Robin Hood and Maid Marian), wrote in the first Act:

…but Hope
Smiles from the threshold of the year to come,
Whispering 'it will be happier;'

If you believe you are suffering from PTSD, or know someone you love who may be, there is hope for living a full and normal life by overcoming the symptoms. Our goal with this guide is to explain, in the simplest of terms, the steps that may be required for a healthy path of healing.

If you have any feedback or recommendations for this or any of our books, please write to us at: MommaBird@BabyBirdGuide.com

A Message from the Author

If you've ever searched for resources related to the impact of mental trauma and stress, you may have been overwhelmed by the vastness of the available information. And yet, despite all these choices, patients frequently report that they have difficulty finding content tailored to them. Websites for Posttraumatic Stress Disorder (PTSD) can be hard to navigate and long texts provide an overwhelming amount of knowledge. Likewise, patients express frustration at the level of psychology jargon, wishing to hear things explained in language that they can comprehend.

Whether you are the trauma survivor, family member, or even a close friend, the purpose of The BabyBird Guide to Stress Disorders is to provide you with an improved understanding of stress disorders, including: trauma, PTSD, and, most importantly, what you can do to help yourself. My biggest hope is to provide just that...hope. What I have found in my work as a licensed clinical psychologist is that although hope is often in short supply, it is critical to moving forward. Hope involves believing that you can feel better; understanding that feeling distress may be a normal reaction to an abnormal situation; and recognizing that you can use the strength that helped you survive the trauma(s) to help yourself recover.

There is hope.

DR HEATHER SILVIO

2 TRAUMA OCCURS IN MANY PLACES AND WAYS

Trauma conjures very different images for everyone. What is deemed traumatic for one person is not necessarily traumatic for another. At its core, however, trauma likely represents pain for the individual experiencing the event, whether physical, emotional, or both. Although more details will be forthcoming about trauma in the later section about the diagnostic criteria for Posttraumatic Stress Disorder (PTSD), the key point is that there is no one definition of what makes something traumatic.

An additional important point is to consider what happens when an individual experiences multiple traumas. It may be traumatic enough to survive a deadly tornado, armed robbery, or combat. Imagine then, that after surviving this trauma, something additional occurs, such as surviving a rape, motor vehicle accident, or earthquake.

Multiple traumas can compound the symptoms and difficulties that may develop as a result.

Cycle of Anxiety

Understanding the cycle of anxiety following a trauma(s) is essential to understanding how an individual may develop PTSD. A cycle of anxiety begins when an individual experiences a traumatic event or events that could be considered a shock to the system, both physically and emotionally. This invariably leads to the development of symptoms that cause significant distress. When the anxiety that follows becomes too unpleasant to bear, the affected individual may choose to manage it in a variety of ways that are not ultimately helpful (e.g., alcohol or other drugs, avoidance of trauma reminders). The result of the ineffective coping strategies is that the anxiety inevitably heightens, rather than reduces. The cycle of anxiety may either maintain or actually increase the very symptoms the survivor would like to eliminate.

3 POSTTRAUMATIC STRESS DISORDER

Following a trauma, many individuals may be quick to wonder whether or not they have Posttraumatic Stress Disorder, or PTSD. How common is the diagnosis, really? According to the 5th version of the go-to book for practitioners, the Diagnostic and Statistical Manual of Mental Disorders (DSM-5, 2013), there is only an 8.7% lifetime risk of developing PTSD for residents of the United States, with the rates of PTSD outside of the US even lower, between 0.5-1.0%.

According to the DSM-5, rates of PTSD are higher in individuals with high-risk occupations, like active duty service members, veterans, and emergency personnel. In particular, individuals who have served in combat, especially those who have been taken captive, have rates as high as 50%. The term "subthreshold PTSD" is applied more often to those who have symptoms causing distress, but not in sufficient quantity and/or intensity to meet the diagnostic criteria.

Remember that diagnoses are simply labels that the medical establishment has chosen to put on certain collections of symptoms to *assist* in identification and treatment. And yet, while diagnoses are helpful, the specific label of PTSD is not required to receive treatment for the symptoms causing distress. Labels do not define us. We do not require a specific diagnosis to pursue treatment.

Acute Stress Disorder

Before delving into the exact diagnostic criteria for PTSD, another diagnosis deserves mention. Acute Stress Disorder (ASD) is an anxiety disorder that precedes PTSD in that it can be diagnosed three days to one month following a trauma. The diagnostic criteria are basically the same, so if treatment is sought within that timeframe, the diagnosis will often be ASD. The diagnosis converts to PTSD if the symptoms remain longer than one month.

What is PTSD?

This section will delve into the more technical explanation of PTSD, paraphrased from the DSM-5, with a focus on the criteria as applied to ages 6 years and older. PTSD is a collection of symptoms related to anxiety that can develop following a trauma. Although the symptoms often develop relatively soon after, there can be delays of many years. As one might expect, frequency, duration, and intensity of symptoms can change over time. Any additional stress, whether traumatic like a violent crime or simply difficult like losing a job, can increase the anxiety and the symptoms.

The diagnostic criteria are grouped according to similar symptoms. To meet criteria for PTSD, there must first be exposure to a trauma followed by symptoms of intrusion or re-experiencing, avoidance, development of negative emotions/thoughts, and increased physical arousal.

Trauma

Trauma is defined predominantly as personally experiencing or witnessing actual or threatened violence. Examples of three very different potential traumas are combat, a tornado, and rape. New to the DSM-5 are additional categories of trauma, namely, hearing that a loved one has been traumatized, and repeatedly being exposed to details of someone else's trauma. This latter addition is predominantly intended to capture emergency personnel whose own lives are not typically in direct danger, yet may develop the symptoms from repeatedly seeing the casualties of trauma.

Intrusion or Re-experiencing

One of the five intrusion symptoms, or symptoms of re-experiencing the trauma, is necessary for the diagnosis of PTSD: intrusive thoughts/memories; nightmares/distressing dreams; feeling as though the trauma were actually being relived; intense psychological distress when reminded of the trauma; and/or pronounced physical reactions when reminded of the trauma.

Avoidance

One of two avoidance symptoms is necessary for the diagnosis of PTSD: avoiding (or trying to avoid) memories, thoughts, or feelings related to the trauma; and/or avoiding reminders such as certain people or places that trigger those memories, thoughts, or feelings related to the trauma.

Development of Negative Emotions/Thoughts

Two of seven symptoms of negative emotions/thoughts are necessary for the diagnosis of PTSD: inability to remember part of the trauma, not due to head injury or substance use; global negative beliefs about the self, others, and the world; distorted thoughts about the trauma leading to inappropriate blame of self or others; persistent negative feelings; significantly decreased interest in activities; feeling detached or alienated from others; and/or an inability to experience positive feelings.

Increased Physical Arousal

Two of six symptoms of increased physical arousal are necessary for the diagnosis of PTSD: irritability; reckless/self-destructive behavior; hypervigilance (overly heightened awareness of surroundings); exaggerated startle response (jumpy); difficulty concentrating /focusing; and/or disturbed sleep.

So, in order to meet criteria for PTSD, an individual must first have a minimum of seven symptoms (including the specific trauma) distributed as discussed above. In addition, these symptoms must be causing some type of distress or negative impact on the individual's life. Finally, the symptoms can't be due to a substance (whether prescribed or not) or to another medical condition. The latter can be a complicating factor in cases where, for example, an active duty service member or veteran received a traumatic brain injury (TBI) since some of the above listed symptoms could be a result of such an injury.

Also new to the DSM-5, is a "specifier", meaning that if an individual meets criteria for PTSD, the diagnosing provider is to also specify whether the individual is experiencing significant dissociation symptoms. Basically, it's a fancy word for two more fancy words: depersonalization and derealization. This specifier is used to denote the feeling of being outside of one's body, or that the world is not real in some way.

Could I have PTSD? A Summary Checklist

If all of the above still feels overwhelming when determining whether or not you meet criteria for PTSD, the following checklist may be helpful:

Have you experienced trauma as defined above?

Do you have one of the five symptoms of re-experiencing the trauma:
• unwanted thoughts
• nightmares
• reliving the trauma
• physical distress when reminded of the trauma
• physiological distress when reminded of the trauma?

Do you have one of the two avoidance symptoms:
• memories, thoughts, or feelings related to the trauma
• avoiding reminders that trigger memories, thoughts, or feelings related to the trauma?

Do you have two of the seven symptoms related to negative emotions and thoughts:
- inability to remember parts of the trauma
- global negative beliefs
- inappropriate blame of self or others for the trauma
- persistent negative feelings
- decreased interest in activities
- feeling detached from others
- inability to experience positive feelings?

Do you have two of the six symptoms of increased physical arousal:
- irritability
- recklessness
- hypervigilance
- jumpiness
- difficulty concentrating
- disturbed sleep?

Are the above symptoms causing significant distress or interfering in your life?

Are the symptoms above solely due to a substance or another medical condition?

You may be wondering what to make of your results. Remember that this is merely a guide and not a clinical diagnosis. A licensed medical or mental health professional needs to assess you to determine whether or not the diagnosis is appropriate. However, based on what you checked above, if you feel like you may meet criteria for PTSD, or if you are experiencing significant distress from your identified symptoms, you have options. In a later chapter of this book, Specific Techniques to Try, tools and techniques are provided to help you minimize the impact of your symptoms. If you feel that you could benefit from professional treatment, please schedule an appointment with a licensed mental health professional.

Associated Symptoms

In addition to the specific symptoms required for an official diagnosis, there are multiple associated symptoms that, while not included technically in the diagnostic criteria, certainly occur with enough frequency to warrant their mention here, namely: suicidal ideation, self-medication, and co-occurring disorders.

Suicidal ideation involves having active thoughts of self-harm and/or feeling that the world would be better off without you in it. Because the symptoms of PTSD can be so challenging to manage and can wreak such havoc on employment and relationships, a feeling that there is no light at the end of the tunnel may begin to develop. A profound sense of helplessness, or that things will never change may lead to suicidal ideation.

In addition, because the symptoms of PTSD can be so hard to live with, the misuse of prescribed drugs or self-medicating with non-prescribed substances like alcohol or other drugs may occur. Because PTSD is an anxiety disorder, an individual with the diagnosis may find that the only way to feel calm or "normal" is by chemically inducing the feelings.

Individuals diagnosed with PTSD are also more likely to have another mental health disorder, including: substance use disorder, depression, or another anxiety disorder.

Although they may not be part of a formal diagnosis, these associated symptoms are noteworthy because they may also be contributing factors to the Cycle of PTSD Anxiety. Be assured, however, that the distress-causing associated symptoms can be reduced with treatment.

Is help really needed?

If you've picked up this book for yourself, then likely the short answer is…Yes. If you are not happy with how you are feeling or how you are interacting with the world, trying something new can help. If you've picked up this book out of concern for a loved one or a close friend, the answer is more complicated. You must consider whether the person is prepared to embrace help from you or from anyone else; whether your loved one wants to address the situation and/or make changes. The good news is that there is much you can do for yourself and/or your loved one, so read on!

4 DO YOU SEE YOURSELF IN THE SYMPTOMS OF PTSD?

Reading to this point may still feel a bit technical, so let's put the above symptoms into the everyday language heard from individuals who are either diagnosed with PTSD or who experience subthreshold PTSD. Note that all the techniques mentioned are detailed in the next chapter.

I just feel on edge all of the time.

As PTSD is an anxiety disorder, one of the hallmarks of the diagnosis is a feeling of anxiousness; described by many as tense, edgy, or restless. Without becoming too technical, these feelings are due to the constant activation of the body in preparation for response to a perceived threat. Following a traumatic event, an individual's basic sense of security and belief that the world is a safe place has been threatened. As a result, an individual may constantly be on the lookout for the next threat. This can be seen, for example, in the PTSD symptom of hypervigilance, which involves constantly scanning the environment for danger. An exaggerated startle response is another PTSD symptom, where any unexpected sensory input such as a loud noise can trigger extreme fear. The single best way to begin to address that physical edginess is to relax. Though this may seem easier said than done, there are multiple techniques that can aid in accomplishing a more relaxed state, including Relaxation Breathing, Muscle Relaxation, and Relaxation Visualization. Each of these relaxation techniques can be used alone or in combination with each other.

Every single day, I'm haunted by thoughts or memories of the trauma(s).

Intrusive thoughts, memories, and images can be considerably distressing. Clearly, if you feel unable to shake these intrusions, your level of distress can increase. There are techniques that can be used to reduce them, involving Thought Stopping followed by Self-talk.

I haven't slept more than four hours a night since the trauma(s).

Disturbed sleep is one of the biggest concerns for individuals diagnosed with PTSD. Sleep disturbance comes in many forms and can be experienced as an individual symptom or in combination, namely: difficulty falling asleep and staying asleep, restless sleep, and bad dreams/nightmares. Improving sleep involves a review of Good Sleep Habits and then Correcting Disturbed Sleep.

I find myself getting angry all the time, over the littlest things.

Let's consider everything we've covered until now. If you feel on edge, jumping at every noise, chronically sleep deprived, and emotionally assaulted by intrusive thoughts and memories, what do you think that will do for your stress level and your ability to manage frustrations? Exactly! On a scale of 1-10 for irritation/anger, it won't take very much at all to shoot you straight up to a 10. After being almost primed to become angry, you may then find yourself easily triggered by anything that feels like an emotional or physical threat. What can you do about it?

Management of anger is very similar to management of anxiety. And since being on edge can easily lead to an anger response, the first step is to relax. Whichever relaxation technique(s) worked for you with anxiety will almost certainly also apply for when you find yourself in an anger-inducing situation. While the relaxation practice(s) will not eliminate the anger, it may decrease the intensity and give you the emotional space to do the second step, Questioning the Angry Response. Most of the time, anger is a natural response to a specific situation. The intensity and the duration of the emotion may signal whether or not it's an anger management problem. Beyond questioning the angry response, you can also use Physical Exercise to release the built-up energy.

I hardly ever leave my house, I have few friends, and I feel like a recluse.

In an effort to avoid the symptoms of anxiety while decreasing the chances of an angry confrontation, many individuals diagnosed with PTSD circumvent the people, places, and things that they believe are likely to trigger those reactions. Learning to Control Distressing Symptoms, followed by deliberately engaging in Exposure Exercises to the people, places, and things you've been shunning, may decrease avoidance tendencies.

Is there anything else I can do to feel better?

Yes! Hopefully you recognize that relaxation exercises and self-talk are critical to decreasing PTSD symptoms. An additional useful tool is a Thought Record. This technique may assist with the management of nearly all of the distressing symptoms of PTSD. Tracking how often a particular symptom occurs may allow you to link your specific thoughts to a given symptom. Using self-talk to challenge and change those thoughts will likely result in helping to achieve the goal of symptom reduction.

5 SPECIFIC TECHNIQUES TO TRY

After reading the diagnostic criteria for PTSD, you may have felt somewhat demoralized given the breadth of symptom clusters that can develop following exposure to a trauma. Hopefully, the described techniques below will reduce the frequency, intensity, and duration of many of the symptoms, whether you meet criteria for a diagnosis of PTSD or not. With effort, you can experience significant reductions in stress, equaling tremendous improvement in functioning and life satisfaction. Remember, however, that the goal is not symptom elimination, but symptom management. This point cannot be overemphasized enough. Despite all of the hard work in therapy, there will be remaining symptoms. Having PTSD, or subthreshold PTSD, will remain a part of who you are for the rest of your life. However, with assistance, you can take back control and manage the symptoms successfully. This next section will detail the tools and techniques that are effective against the symptoms of PTSD.

Relaxation Breathing

The single-most effective technique for the largest number of people is relaxation breathing. Based on feedback received, this relaxation method seems to work best because it is simple in concept, relatively easy to remember, does not draw attention to the person doing it, and acts quickly upon the body to reduce physical symptoms of distress such as elevated heart rate and muscle tension. There are different types of relaxation breathing. Two recommended techniques that have proven results are deep breathing and diaphragmatic breathing.

Deep breathing is fairly basic, involving a four count breath inhaled through the nose, followed by a four count breath exhaled through the mouth. Repeat 10 times. The breaths are not that different in comparison to the normal depth of breathing. In other words, this relaxation breathing technique should not necessarily be noticeable to others. For the first couple of weeks, try practicing the series of breaths six times per day; when waking, mid-morning, lunchtime, mid-afternoon, dinnertime, and bedtime. This effort will help the mind and body become used to this type of breathing as habitual, before attempting to use it specifically in response to an anxious situation.

Diaphragmatic breathing employs the diaphragm to push air in and out of the lungs. To get comfortable with the technique, lie down, and place one hand on your chest, the other hand on your stomach. Breathe, while focusing on making your stomach rise with each inhalation; this lets you know that you are using your diaphragm. Once you feel assured that you are doing it effectively, you can do it anywhere, anytime, in any position. Try practicing this type of breathing for 3-5 minutes, several times per day, before attempting to use it specifically in response to an anxious situation.

Sometimes a combination of the two breathing techniques works best. Once one or both become habitual, start using them directly when feeling anxious. These breathing methods are especially useful when actively confronting the tendency to avoid triggering the exhausting nature of hypervigilance and intrusive thoughts.

Muscle Relaxation

Muscle relaxation involves systematically tightening and releasing the muscles of the body. Work with groups of muscles sequentially, or by beginning at one end of the body and moving towards the opposite end. By releasing the muscles after tightening them, the body is helped to recognize and remember what relaxed feels like. This technique also assists the body in reabsorbing the chemicals that may have been released in preparation to a response of threat.

Relaxation Visualization

Relaxation visualization is creating in your mind a location where you feel happy, or at least safe and comfortable. The location can be a recreation from your memory, it can be an existing place, or it can be something wholly created in your imagination. The key to making this practice work is to engage all of the senses when creating the location. The beach can be a good choice for this technique as it is often associated with peace and a more relaxing time. Imagine the beach with crystal clear water and white sand; smell the suntan lotion and salt water; taste the lemonade you're drinking; hear the seagulls overhead and the waves crashing to shore; feel the sand between your toes and the wind on your skin. Can you picture the beach? By engaging all of your senses, the image has a realness to it that might otherwise be lacking. When you find yourself feeling anxious, you can use the cue word "beach" to immediately feel enveloped by the sense of calm that your visualization brings.

Thought Stopping

Thought stopping is used as a first step in reducing intrusive thoughts of traumatic events. When triggering occurs, meaning that something in the present is pulling you to the past, and an intrusive thought, memory, or image is the result, the first thing you can do is to simply tell yourself, "Stop". Used either silently or aloud, by simply interrupting the connection in the brain between the triggering event and the intrusion, you begin to weaken that connection. Could using such a technique result in the thoughts becoming resistant? (For example, try unthinking "pink elephant".) That absolutely can be the case, which is why it typically is most effective to couple thought stopping with self-talk to challenge why you're having the intrusive thought in the first place.

Self-talk

Self-talk is exactly what it sounds like. These are the internal thoughts you tell yourself in any given situation. When you find yourself triggered and an intrusive thought, memory, or image enters your mind, begin with, "Stop". After you interrupt that connection, follow up with self-talk aimed at challenging the presence of the thought, the memory, or the image. This is not the time to berate yourself for having the negative thought or image; it's a time to be compassionate with yourself.

Some examples of statements you could make to yourself include: "I've just been triggered"; "This thought, memory, or image is of an event from the past and I can leave it in the past"; and "There is no threat here".

Much like with the relaxation techniques described above, the use of thought stopping plus self-talk works best with consistent practice. Do your best to try this every single time you experience an intrusive thought, memory, or image. Over time, you will likely notice that you don't need to use the techniques as often. The connections between triggers and intrusive thoughts, memories, and images will weaken from disuse.

Good Sleep Habits

Good sleep habits are critical to improving sleep. Addressing the symptoms of PTSD that interfere with sleep may have no effect if you are unknowingly sabotaging your sleep with poor sleep practices. Good sleep habits can be global as well as specific, and actually start when you first wake up.

During the course of your day, be aware of what you consume. Alcohol, nicotine, caffeine, and certain medications can all interfere with sleep. Alcohol consumption may help you fall asleep, but can result in fractured sleep. Caffeine can take up to 12 hours to leave the system. Nicotine, although it may help you feel relaxed, is actually a stimulant (meaning it will keep you awake). The side effects of many prescribed medications may disrupt sleep. Additionally, avoid heavy meals within a couple of hours before bedtime. Do, however, have a snack before bed so that your body doesn't go into searching-for-food mode in the middle of the night.

Avoid taking naps. If you feel like you can't get through the day without one, keep it under an hour and no later than midday. Napping can upset your sleep rhythms. When you try to go to bed at night, your mind and body may become confused.

As bedtime gets closer, give yourself plenty of time to unwind from the day before trying to go to sleep. Engage in a low-key activity like reading (not watching the news!) so that you truly feel ready for bed. Use the bed for sleep and sex only. Do not go to bed until you are honestly tired and not just telling yourself you should sleep. Make sure the temperature, noise level, and mattress comfort are good.

Correcting Disturbed Sleep

You may find falling asleep difficult due to a frantic mind that won't shut off. The good sleep habit of unwinding from the day can assist with that because it gives you the opportunity to release the worries of the day. Use of relaxation techniques before bedtime can also be especially helpful; Relaxation Breathing, Muscle Relaxation, and Relaxation Visualization can work, alone or in combination.

If you aren't asleep within twenty minutes or so (don't watch the clock!), get out of bed. Yes, get out of bed and do something really boring like reading the telephone book until your eyelids begin to droop. Get back into bed. If you are still not asleep within about twenty minutes, repeat this process until you are. You may find at first that you are getting in and out of bed multiple times each night. Have confidence that if you are consistent, over time this number will decrease.

If you wake up before you want to, assess what woke you. If it's something that you can take care of quickly and return to bed, like going to the bathroom or getting a glass of water, that's fine. On the other hand, if the awakening is due to a nightmare or bad dream, there are steps you can take. Note: if you've noticed you have trouble reorienting yourself upon first awakening, use a small night light to provide enough illumination to see clearly, but not so bright to become a distraction. When you first wake up from a nightmare, you are liable to feel residual negative emotions. Immediately tell yourself that it was just a nightmare and that you are safe in bed. Engage then in relaxation breathing, muscle relaxation, and/or relaxation visualization to assist with returning to sleep. If you are not able to fall back asleep within about twenty minutes, follow the guidelines above. Remember that it may seem like you are getting in and out of bed a lot, but this will decrease with consistent use.

Repeating nightmares may be treated with Imagery Rehearsal Therapy; a specific therapy that was largely developed by Dr. Barry Krakow, MD, a board certified sleep disorder specialist. A modified version of this therapeutic technique has been successfully used with combat veterans. It can also be used for individuals with non-combat trauma:

1.   Write down your dream using as many sensory descriptions as possible. What do you see, smell, and hear? Capture the anxiety-provoking components of the nightmare, but don't overlook the mundane details.

2.   Rewrite the nightmare, changing multiple components. For example, being chased in a dark alley by a man with a gun becomes being followed in a sunny park by a friendly dog with a ball.

3.   Rehearse the dream throughout the day, especially before bedtime.

4.   Continue to rehearse the dream in your mind until the nightmare has changed to match the rewritten version.

Questioning the Angry Response

Challenge the thoughts that maintain your anger in three steps:

1.   Question whether or not anger is an appropriate response and if it is at the appropriate level of response. Ask yourself, "Is it worth it?"

2.   Consider alternative perspectives. If an interpersonal situation has triggered your anger, it can be particularly helpful to consider the other person's perspective. Ask yourself, "What is another way of looking at this situation?"

3.   Move into problem solving mode. Initially, you may find that walking away is your best option for avoiding verbal and/or physical altercations. This is fine as a short-term management technique, but you'll want to move in the direction of modifying your thoughts to create and maintain long-term change. Consider what you are hoping to accomplish and the most productive way to get there. Anger is often counterproductive to what we're hoping to accomplish. Ask yourself, "What are my goals in this situation?"

Remember that while you may notice improvement right away, the techniques of anger management take consistent practice to become habitual.

Physical Exercise

Most likely you already know exercise is good for you. Engaging in physical activity to burn off the excess energy related to anger can be an excellent way to feel better. Use this technique after leaving the anger-inducing situation as the exercise may reduce pent up energy and allow you to think more clearly. It can also be used to release anger and as a preventative measure to reduce the overall edginess that leads to the angry response.

Control Distressing Symptoms

In your efforts to decrease avoidance, the first step is to learn to control the distressing symptoms of anger and anxiety that result. You can practice the techniques presented specifically for reducing anxiety and anger, including Relaxation Breathing, Muscle Relaxation, Relaxation Visualization, Thought Stopping, Self-talk, and Questioning the Angry Response. When you feel that you have better control of the distressing symptoms themselves, you may be ready to begin venturing out again; to see the people and places you had been avoiding, through use of Exposure Exercises.

Exposure Exercises

What you've likely noticed is that you avoid very specific people, places, or things that you believe are likely to trigger anxiety and/or anger. You may be able to go to work or school, but other locations with unfamiliar people may be too much. Once you've made the decision to expose yourself to those trigger situations, start slowly and build up. For example, perhaps you have difficulty going to the grocery store during rush hour because of all of the people on the roads, in the parking lot, and in the store. Don't just jump in at that level. Take baby steps to build your confidence in your ability. Here is a step by step example of how you could accomplish your goal:

1. Pick a less busy time to go to the store. Try going in the middle of the night first or the middle of the day, before going during rush hour.

2. Drive into the parking lot. If you don't experience any anxiety, you can move to the next step. If you do experience anxiety, use your relaxation exercise and self-talk to keep physical symptoms under control, reminding yourself there is no threat. Once you are able to drive into the parking lot without anxiety, move onto the next step.

3. Park the car in the parking lot. If you don't experience any anxiety, you can move to the next step. If you do experience anxiety, use your relaxation exercise and self-talk as described in step 2. Once you are able to park without anxiety, move onto the next step.

4. Walk up to the door. If you don't experience any anxiety, you can move to the next step. Otherwise, use your techniques until you no longer experience anxiety and can move to the next step.

5. Walk around the store without buying anything. If you don't experience any anxiety, you can move to the next step. Otherwise, use your techniques until you no longer experience anxiety and can move to the next step.

6.   Actually shop. Even at this step, you may find it helpful to buy only one or two items the first time. Continue to build up to a full shopping trip.

Although this takes time, eventually you will reach your goal. And when you do, one of two things can happen: this success will help you feel more comfortable and will spread to other anxiety- or anger-inducing situations without much additional work, or, you may find you have to repeat this series of steps in other situations. Either way, you are likely to find that your list of avoided people and places dwindles more and more until you reach the point at which you are satisfied.

Thought Record

Thought Records serve multiple purposes. First, they offer a method for tracking symptoms to notice any patterns that exist. Maybe you become angrier in the morning or experience more anxiety after dark. Second, they allow you to increase awareness of which emotions, behaviors, and thoughts are linked together. Third, they provide an organized way to directly challenge the symptom-maintaining thoughts. Here's how they work:

1.   When you notice an increase in any negative emotion, take out a piece of paper or a small notepad. To improve accuracy of thought awareness, do this as close to the moment as safely possible.

2. Immediately note three things on the paper: situational details (date/time/what's actually happening), emotional details (feelings and intensity, on a scale of 1-10), and thoughts. Ask yourself, "What is going through my mind right now?"

3. Challenge those identified thoughts as discussed above under Self-talk and Questioning the Angry Response, taking note of new thoughts that may develop, and any changes in emotion and/or intensity. To notice patterns and to begin the decrease of some of the negative reactions, keep this Thought Record for at least two weeks.

6 NOBODY EXISTS IN A VACUUM

While you may sometimes feel isolated, or choose to remain isolated, as a result of the symptoms you're experiencing, you still exist as a citizen in the world. Perhaps you have a spouse or significant other, children, parents, and/or other close family and friends. Or it may simply mean that you have surface relationships in your day-to-day life with people such as a neighbor, store clerk, supervisor, and/or teacher. Although both deep and surface relationships are ultimately important, this section will focus on the deeper relationships that have the potential to help you recover.

Communicating with Family and Friends

Developing effective communication with your immediate family and close friends is the first important step. Following a trauma, you may find that it's harder to relate to the people around you than it was before. Having experienced a physical threat and/or witnessed truly life and death situations, it may be difficult to make small talk, to explain what you experienced, and to communicate when you are overwhelmed by the people around you. While the people in your life may have experienced stressful, even highly difficult situations, it is unlikely that they've experienced your specific trauma(s), and as such have no real understanding of what you've been through. They may repeatedly ask for information about the experiences that you have no interest in reliving. They may not understand why your feelings and behaviors have changed. "Why can't you move on?" may become an unspoken, or even spoken, refrain. Being able to communicate how you feel is critical to maintaining those connections with family.

There are a number of online resources to help you learn how to communicate effectively to the people you love, including:

MyPTSD Forum:

> https://www.myptsd.com/c/forums/ptsd-relationships.21/

UK's Mental Healthy:

> http://www.mentalhealthy.co.uk/anxiety/ptsd/the-effects-of-ptsd-on-relationship.html

Consult a therapist if talking it through with someone feels like the best solution for you.

Be Wary of Isolation

Beyond communication, it is important to remain part of the family and the wider community. Be careful not to isolate yourself through avoidance. Avoidance is a defining characteristic of PTSD because you feel better when you avoid the situations that may trigger anxiety and/or anger. However, if you are constantly telling your spouse, children, and/or other close family members that you can't participate in activities with them, this can become a negative cycle from which it is hard to break free. Normal or typical activities will bring familiarity to you every day. Go to the park, a place of worship, and the grocery store. Participate in neighborhood events, volunteer at a local charity, and play on a community sports team. The specific activities are not important. What is important is to remain involved so that you don't lose your connection to the rest of humanity. If that happens, it can be much harder to come back, though certainly not impossible.

Allow Loved Ones to Be Involved

Loved ones will want to support you and may ask what they can do to help. If you are the one who has suffered the trauma(s), you may want to be ready with ideas on how the people around you can participate in your healing path. Consider asking them to educate themselves on PTSD and ask them to conduct their own research. Remind them that although they can be a part of your healing, only you can forge your path. Ask them to be patient.

7 LET'S BOTTOM LINE IT

Does all of this mean I'm broken?

Absolutely not, though the sentiment is often commonly heard. Perhaps you feel that nobody can help or that the symptoms wouldn't have happened had you been stronger. Maybe you think that you are too old to make changes. Developing symptoms of PTSD, whether diagnosed or not, has nothing to do with being weak or broken or old. Think of some of the tactics that helped you survive the trauma. On a deployment, for example, being super aware of the surroundings, not sleeping soundly so that you can respond to changes immediately, seeing things in black and white, and expecting others to get it right the first time are skills that kept you alive. Or, while surviving a rape, emotionally leaving your body, fighting any unexpected touch, and watching for a chance to escape to safety are all part of your survival instinct.

All of these are natural reactions that protected you in life and death situations. They don't, however, work so well in the daily world. This doesn't mean that you are broken. It just means you need to retrain your mind and body to recognize that it's no longer necessary to act as though you're still in a dangerous setting. There are four keys to remember:

1. Many symptoms may resolve on their own; others may require a little or a lot of work. That's okay. Recovery is a lifelong process, partly because when other stresses in your life increase, the symptoms of PTSD may also increase. Being aware of this possibility will help reduce the impact when it happens.

2. You have a lot more control than you think. You don't have control over other people, and you actually have limited control over your environment, but you ultimately have total control over your choices. This includes how you choose to think, feel, and behave. If you truly practice the tools and techniques contained in this book, over time you will experience reduced symptoms. Unfortunately, it is impossible to predict how long it may take. Some techniques may reduce symptoms the same day. Others may take a couple of weeks or months of repetition to be fully effective.

3. You don't have to go it alone. In addition to having a trusted family member or friend to discuss things with, you can always seek professional help. There is no shame in accessing these resources. It takes a strong person to ask for help.

4. Remember, don't ever give up! No matter how overwhelming a particular situation or symptom may feel, it is temporary and can be managed. You just have to keep trying different approaches until you find what works for you. You can manage your symptoms to move forward and live the happy, productive life that you want and deserve.

Have hope.

DR HEATHER SILVIO

8 FURTHER READING & RESOURCES

American Psychiatric Association: Diagnostic and Statistical Manual of Mental Disorders, Fifth Edition. Arlington, VA, American Psychiatric Association, 2013.

Military OneSource:
    http://www.militaryonesource.mil/

US Department of Veteran Affairs: National Center for PTSD
    http://www.ptsd.va.gov/

UK Military Health Services
    http://www.nhs.uk/NHSEngland/Militaryhealthcar e/Pages/Militaryhealthcare.aspx

ABOUT THE AUTHOR

Dr. Heather Silvio is a licensed clinical psychologist. working on a clinical team for the Combat Related PTSD Treatment Program at the Department of Veterans Affairs in Las Vegas. A veteran herself, she was previously a Lieutenant Commander in the United States Public Health Service. Heather is the author of the self-help book/program *Happiness by the Numbers: 9 Steps to Authentic Happiness,* the romantic comedy *Not Quite Famous: A Romantic Comedy of an Actress on the Edge,* the short story/poetry collection *Beyond the Abyss: Tales of the Supernatural,* and the psychological thriller/murder mystery *Courting Death.* She is also an award-winning screenwriter, actress, and dancer. She lives with her wonderful husband, Sidney, and their cats, Snowball and Daphne.

To check out all this and more, as well as sign up for Heather's monthly newsletter, visit http://www.heathersilvio.com.

Made in the USA
Columbia, SC
11 October 2017